T0145172

LET
HIM
USE
YOU

Written by Tonya Nalls, P.h.D.

illustrated by Courtney Monday

AuthorHouse™
1663 Liberty Drive
Bloomington, IN 47403
www.authorhouse.com
Phone: 833-262-8899

This book is printed on acid-free paper.

ISBN: 978-1-6655-5838-9 (sc)
ISBN: 978-1-6655-5969-0 (hc)
ISBN: 978-1-6655-5839-6 (e)

Print information available on the last page.

Published by AuthorHouse 07/20/2023

authorHOUSE®

THIS bOOK bELOngs to:

....

This book is dedicated to my grandchildren, Christopher, Camille, Skylar, and Chase. You all are beautiful, talented, and uniquely made. Remember to always use your talents to advance the Kingdom of God. For it is through you that God demonstrates his love for others. I love you all to the moon and back.

In urban communities, "Let him use you" is not an unusual phrase to hear, but often it's no more than a saying. Most people who use this phrase for effect, do not believe that God can really use them.

Often, their desire to be used by God is overshadowed by a negative self-image, derogatory opinions of others, or lack of ability. The good news is, God specializes in transforming those individuals into great leaders of their time. Allow me to introduce a few to you.

PETER had a temper,
but God used him.

He served as the head of apostles and was the first to perform a miracle.

JONAH ran from God. He was human and suffered from self-doubt, but God used him to demonstrate his mercy and love by preaching to others.

GIDEON was insecure, but God used him as a mighty warrior.

Miriam was a gossiper but was chosen by God to be a prophetess. She led the Israelites in the song of the sea, after Pharaoh's army was destroyed at the sea of reeds. Through her we learned that a small act of bravery can change the course of our lives, and the lives of others.

Martha was a worrier, but God chose her as the patron saint of servants and cooks.

She was the picture of hospitality and the recipient of a miracle from Jesus as she was the sister of Lazarus, whom Jesus raised from the dead.

THOMAS was a doubter. He doubted the resurrection of Jesus and demanded physical proof of the wounds of Christ's Crucifixion.

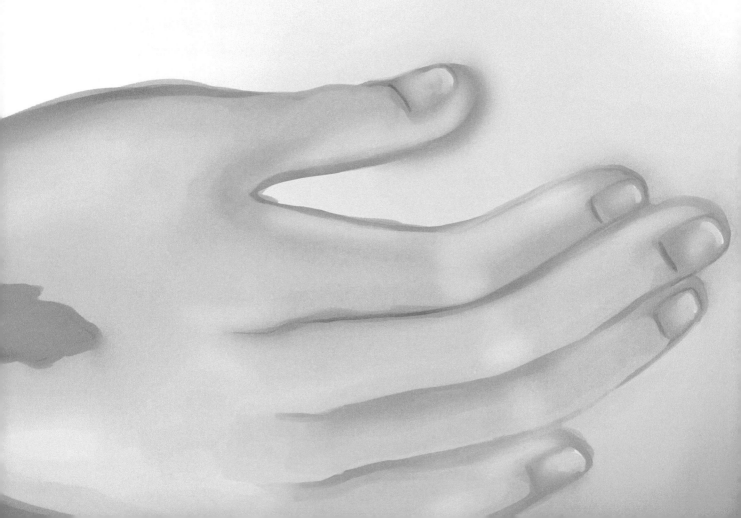

So, God made sure that he became the first person to acknowledge the divinity of Jesus. No more "doubting Thomas."

SARA was impatient, but God changed her name and made her a mother of nations.

ELIJAH was moody yet used by God to resurrect the dead, bring down fire from the sky and to lead a school of prophets.

MOSES stuttered yet he led God's people
out of slavery in Egypt to the Promised Land.

God even gave him special powers to perform other acts of leadership.

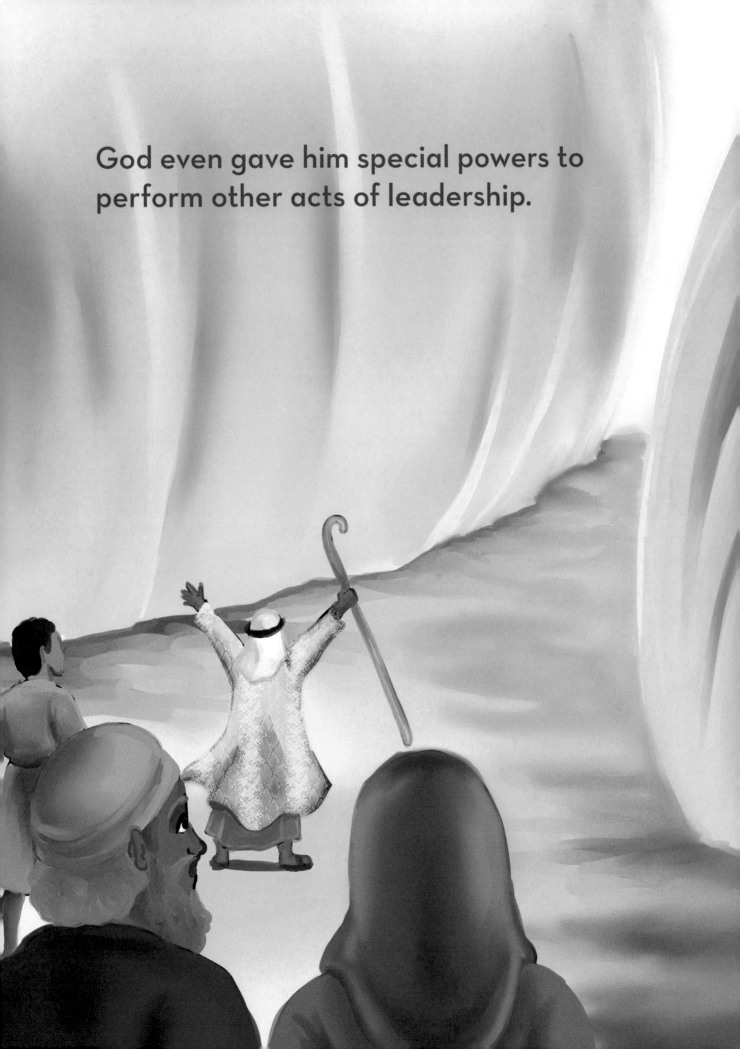

ZACCHEUS was a short, dishonest man whose curiosity led him to Jesus and salvation. He also became one of Jesus' disciples.

ABRAHAM was old. God called him to leave his country and his people and journey to an undesignated land. He became the founder of a new nation and is seen as the "father of faith."

God used Peter, Jonah, Gideon, Miriam, Martha, Thomas, Sara, Elijah, Moses, Zaccheus, Abraham and he can use YOU too.